PREFACE

This report is a companion piece to an annotated bibliography on the subject of the behavioral characteristics of U.S. investors. The primary goal of the report is to identify common investment mistakes and to provide scholarly commentary from university professors and professionals in the fields of economics, business, finance, psychology, and sociology. The secondary goal is to provide insights into how investors make the initial decision to invest and why some are reluctant to invest at all. Many of the scholars cited here have made seminal contributions to the analysis of the human element of investing. Students of their work can learn much about the patterns and pitfalls associated with investor behavior.

Although the citation for each research study includes a URL directly accessing the article described, most of the URLs link to fee-based, subscriber databases. In general, the cited articles are available via a number of these vendor databases, such as JSTOR, EBSCO, ProQuest, NBER, or Wiley Interscience. The citation for each abstract also provides a URL linking to a Web site that offers free access to the article, such as a faculty Web site or other online source, if such a link is available. However, the Federal Research Division is unable to guarantee the stability of these additional links.

TABLE OF CONTENTS

FIGURES

OVERVIEW

According to statistical evidence presented in academic studies, patterns of investor behavior are often counterproductive. Drawing on a comprehensive review of academic journal articles, reporting research in the relatively new field of behavioral finance, this paper examines patterns of investor behavior, as well as reasons that individuals are reluctant to invest in the first place. The "Annotated Bibliography on the Behavioral Characteristics of U.S. Investors," also prepared by the Federal Research Division, summarizes the research cited in this paper.

THE ROLE OF BEHAVIORAL FINANCE

Pioneers of the field of behavioral finance set out to challenge the prevailing assumptions of rational expectations theory, which holds that investors act rationally and in their self-interest, aiming to maximize returns at a given level of risk. Behavioral finance adherents emphasize the social, cognitive, or emotional factors that lead investors to depart from the rational behavior that traditional economists assume. As University of California finance professors Brad M. Barber and Terrance Odean explain in their article on "The Courage of Misguided Convictions," behavioral finance incorporates "observable, systematic, and very human departures into standard models of financial markets."[1]

Behavioral finance holds that investors tend to fall into predictable patterns of destructive behavior. In other words, they make the same mistakes repeatedly. Specifically, many investors damage their portfolios by underdiversifying; trading frequently; following the herd; favoring the familiar (domestic stocks, company stock, and glamour stocks); selling winning positions and holding onto losing positions (disposition effect); and succumbing to optimism, short-term thinking, and overconfidence (self-attribution bias).[2]

---

[1] Brad M. Barber and Terrance Odean, "The Courage of Misguided Convictions," *Financial Analysts Journal* 55, no. 6 (November–December 1999): 41–55. Available by subscription from JSTOR, http://www.jstor.org/stable/ 4480208 (accessed December 10, 2009). Also available from http://faculty.haas.berkeley.edu/odean/Papers% 20current%20versions/FAJ%20NovDec99%20Barber%20and%20Odean.pdf (accessed January 15, 2010).

[2] Besides Barber and Odean, some of the major figures in the field of behavioral finance are Nicholas Barberis (Yale), Shlomo Benartzi (UCLA), David Hirshleifer (University of California at Irvine), Daniel Kahneman (Princeton), Andrei Shleifer (Harvard), Richard H. Thaler (University of Chicago), and Robert Vishny (University of Chicago).

Prospect Theory

Behavioral finance is a multidisciplinary field that draws on psychology and sociology to shed light on financial behavior. One of the foundations of behavioral finance is prospect theory, developed by Princeton psychology professor Daniel Kahneman, a Nobel Prize laureate, and the late psychologist Amos Tversky, last affiliated with Stanford University. Prospect theory examines how people maximize value or utility in choosing among alternatives that involve risk. As applied to finance, prospect theory posits that, when measuring utility under conditions of uncertainty, investors pay too much attention to incremental gains and losses. Excessive risk aversion leads them to attach more importance to avoiding losses than to achieving gains. As Figure 1 demonstrates in graphical terms, the value function guiding investors is asymmetrical with respect to losses versus gains.

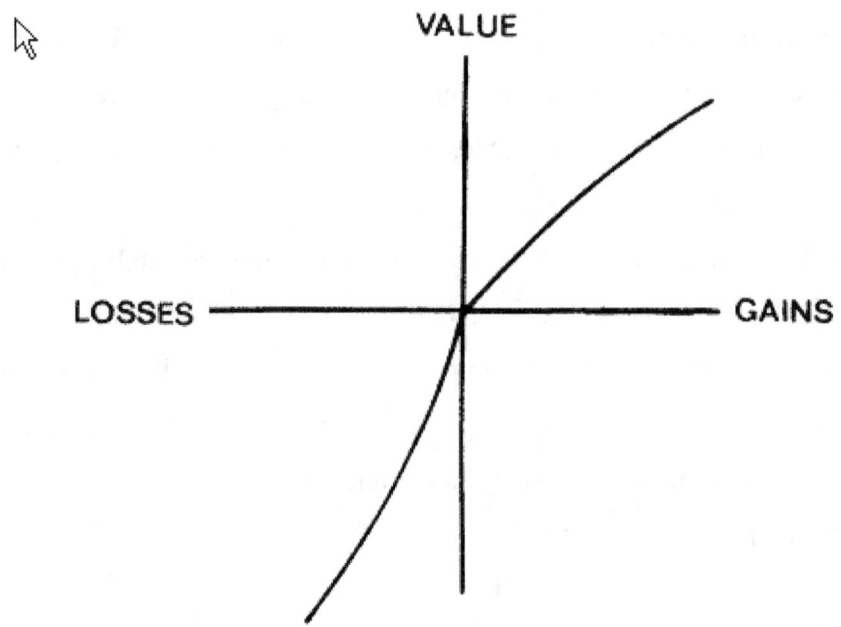

Source: Daniel Kahneman and Amos Tversky, "Prospect Theory: An Analysis of Decision under Risk," *Econometrica* 47, no. 2 (March 1979): 279.

Figure 1. Value Function in Prospect Theory

Consequently, investors realize subpar investment returns, rather than maximizing wealth, as rational expectations theory predicts. In an article on "Aspects of Investor

Psychology," coauthored with Mark W. Riepe, who specializes in investment products and mutual-fund research at Charles Schwab & Company, Kahneman uses prospect theory to highlight biases of judgment—overconfidence, optimism, hindsight, and overreaction to past events—and errors of preference—assigning probabilities and values to future outcomes. These errors and biases lead to poor investment decisions.[3]

Overconfidence

Overconfidence, an emotion common among investors, triggers a wide range of investment errors. In the worst-case outcome, an overconfident investor becomes a victim of some form of investment fraud, such as a Ponzi scheme. In his article, "On Financial Frauds and Their Causes: Investor Overconfidence," Steven Pressman, an economist at Monmouth University, identifies overconfidence as the primary psychological culprit responsible for the susceptibility of otherwise sophisticated investors to financial fraud.[4] Pressman maintains that empirical psychology, which analyzes how people make choices when confronted with uncertainty, offers a better explanation for the success of Ponzi schemes than does neoclassical economics, with its emphasis on the role of asymmetric information in risky situations. Pressman advocates providing the public with more information about the risks of scams, educating potential investors about the details of specific cases of fraud. He also recommends substantially increasing the penalties for such schemes, relative to rewards.

Human Sentiment

Given the role of emotion in investing, some social scientists take a very skeptical view of the stock market in general. In "Money and Sentiment: A Psychodynamic Approach to Behavioral Finance," medical doctor Ildiko Mohacsy, now deceased, and Heidi Lefer, a member of the professional staff of the CUNY Research Council, describe the stock market as a "conglomeration of human sentiment" (hope, fear, and greed) that is not subject to purely

---

[3] Daniel Kahneman and Mark W. Riepe, "Aspects of Investor Psychology," *Journal of Portfolio Management* 24, no. 4 (Summer 1998): 52. Available by subscription: http://find.galegroup.com/gtx/infomark.do?&contentSet=IAC-Documents&type=retrieve&tabID=T002&prodId=ITOF&docId=A21046822&source=gale&srcprod=ITOF&userGroupName=loc_main&version=1.0 (accessed June 29, 2010).
[4] Steven Pressman, "On Financial Frauds and Their Causes: Investor Overconfidence," *American Journal of Economics and Sociology* 57, no. 4 (October 1998): 405–21. Available by subscription from JSTOR, http://www.jstor.org/stable/3487115 (accessed December 10, 2009).

scientific analysis.[5] According to their thesis, investors often engage in wishful or magical thinking rather than logical thinking.

RELUCTANCE TO INVEST

Many people fail to invest at all or neglect to lay an adequate groundwork for satisfactory retirement income. Financial illiteracy and the lack of trust in financial markets play important roles in curbing participation in retirement plans. Therefore, employer-sponsored retirement plans that require opt-in participation often encounter inertia and passivity on the part of employees.

In "Lessons from Behavioral Finance for Retirement Plan Design," Olivia S. Mitchell of the University of Pennsylvania and Stephen P. Utkus of the Vanguard Group summarize the key findings of behavioral finance regarding pension design and structure.[6] First, the article examines the fundamental issue of how people make their initial economic decision to save for retirement. Moving beyond conventional wisdom on the rational allocation of resources over a lifetime, the authors discuss how and why individuals who choose to save make flawed decisions, dependent on the extent of their self-control and on their limited information, time, and cognitive ability ("bounded rationality"). Mitchell and Utkus suggest that choices regarding whether or not to save reflect an individual's subjective discount rate, applied to the time value of money. They designate those individuals who tend to defer consumption in order to save as "exponential discounters," calling those who save little or nothing "hyperbolic discounters." As shown in Figure 2, exponential discounters assign a higher value to future money than hyperbolic discounters do.

---

[5] Ildiko Mohacsy and Heidi Lefer, "Money and Sentiment: A Psychodynamic Approach to Behavioral Finance," *Journal of the American Academy of Psychoanalysis and Dynamic Psychiatry* 35, no. 3 (Fall 2007): 455–75. Available by subscription from a number of vendors, including Proquest, http://proquest.umi.com/login (accessed January 13, 2010).
[6] Olivia S. Mitchell and Stephen P. Utkus, "Lessons from Behavioral Finance for Retirement Plan Design," in *Pension Design and Structure: New Lessons from Behavioral Finance*, ed. Mitchell and Utkus, 3–41 (Oxford, UK: Oxford University Press, 2004).

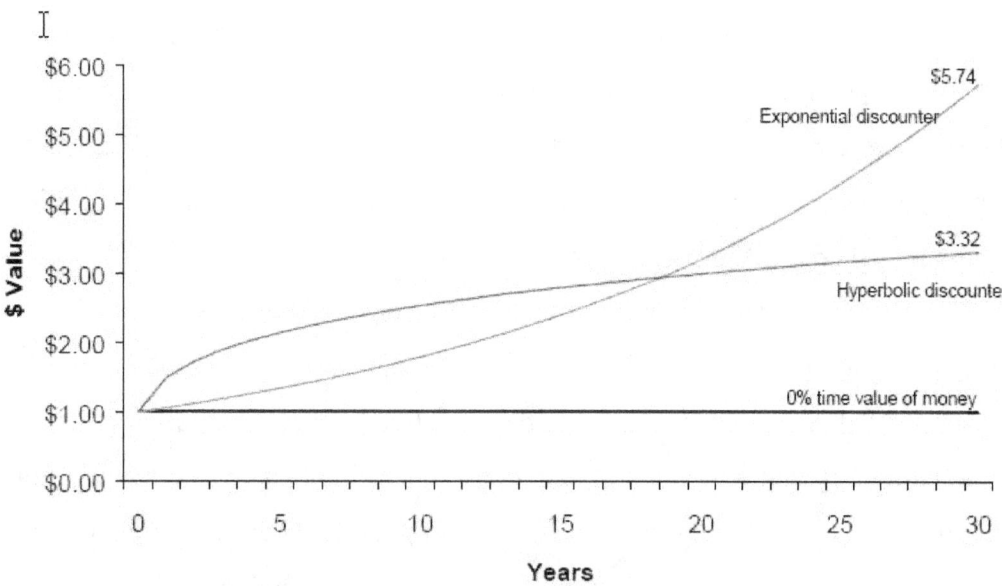

Source: Olivia S. Mitchell and Stephen P. Utkus, "Lessons from Behavioral Finance for Retirement Plan Design," in *Pension Design and Structure: New Lessons from Behavioral Finance*, ed. Mitchell and Utkus, 3–41 (Oxford: Oxord University Press, 2004), 7.

Figure 2. Hyperbolic vs. Exponential Discounting

Behavioral finance theorists also note that conventional economic theory cannot explain the extent to which the design of a retirement plan affects investment decisions. Retirement plans featuring automatic enrollment have much higher participation rates than those in which enrollment is discretionary, because individuals tend to acquiesce in participating and to accept the plan's default options. Furthermore, when a retirement plan's provisions require participants to sign up for (opt into) a retirement plan, individuals tend to procrastinate or to do nothing.

Lack of Financial Literacy

Reluctance to invest in the stock market is often the result of financial illiteracy. In "Financial Literacy and Stock Market Participation," Maarten van Rooij, affiliated with the Dutch Central Bank, Rob Alessie of Utrecht University, and Annamaria Lusardi of Dartmouth College use data from the Netherlands to show that people with low financial literacy are less likely to invest in stocks than those who are financially literate.[7] In fact, financial illiteracy not only correlates with the choice not to invest, but causes it. While most households know about basic financial concepts, such as compound interest, inflation, and the time value of money, very few households understand the more advanced financial concepts often considered necessary for successful investing, such as the difference between stocks and bonds, the inverse relationship of bond prices and interest rates, and risk diversification.

In "Financial Literacy and Planning: Implications for Retirement Wellbeing," Lusardi and Mitchell report widespread financial illiteracy among Americans, particularly among women, minorities, and those without a college degree.[8] Furthermore, the authors find a link between financial literacy and retirement planning. Moreover, financially literate investors who plan for the future tend to use formal tools and methods rather than relying on relatives and coworkers for advice. Since investment success is dependent on planning, wide disparities in household wealth upon retirement, between those who plan and those who do not, are no surprise. The study reveals that, overall, only a minority of households feel confident about the adequacy of their retirement saving. The authors recommend financial education programs targeting the least financially sophisticated segments of the population.

Lack of Trust

Lack of trust is another explanation for the reluctance to invest. In "Trusting the Stock Market," the authors—Luigi Guiso of the European University Institute, Paola Sapienza of Northwestern University, and Luigi Zingales of the University of Chicago—attribute limited participation in the stock market, particularly among wealthy investors, to a lack of trust and to the fear of being cheated by participants in the capital markets.[9] Subjective and cultural factors determine how trusting people are, as well as whether and how much they are willing to invest.

---

[7] Maarten Van Rooij, Annamaria Lusardi, and Rob Alessie, "Financial Literacy and Stock Market Participation" (National Bureau of Economic Research Working Paper 13565, October 2007), http://www.nber.org/papers/w13565 (accessed May 21, 2010).

[8] Annamaria Lusardi and Olivia S. Mitchell, "Financial Literacy and Planning: Implications for Retirement Wellbeing" (Michigan Retirement Research Center Research Paper No. WP 2005-108, December 2005), 1–28, http://papers.ssrn.com/sol3/papers.cfm?abstract_id=881847 (accessed May 24, 2010).

[9] Luigi Guiso, Paola Sapienza, and Luigi Zingales, "Trusting the Stock Market," *Journal of Finance* 63, no. 6 (December 2008): 2557–2600, http://www.bus.wisc.edu/finance/Meyferth/Fedenia/Articles/Guiso%20Sapienza% 20Zingales%202007.pdf (accessed May 19, 2010).

Retirement Saving Inadequacy

Jonathan Skinner, an economics professor at Dartmouth College, uses the life-cycle model to examine the question of whether people are saving enough for retirement, reporting his findings in the article, "Are You Sure You're Saving Enough for Retirement?"[10] The life-cycle model assumes that a person tries to maintain a relatively stable ("smooth") standard of living over the course of his or her lifetime, and that this pattern continues through retirement, when that person draws on savings accumulated during his or her career. Skinner attempts to determine how much nonhousing net worth retired people require to continue smooth consumption. His findings indicate that those who save at high rates during their working lives are accustomed to consuming less and, therefore, do not need as much for retirement. Because they have set aside more, this pattern of saving more and consuming less provides investors with a double dividend. They benefit twice: first from becoming accustomed to a modest standard of living and second from saving more. Therefore, the author recommends saving incrementally more each year. Even if most American households fall short of the targets that the life-cycle model stipulates, they may have lower expenses during retirement—except for health care expenses—and may find that they are able to compensate for inadequate savings by economizing. However, Skinner identifies growing out-of-pocket health-care costs as a cause for concern.

COMMON INVESTMENT MISTAKES

Researchers have identified a number of common investment mistakes and have scrutinized some significant patterns of negative investment behavior. Counterproductive patterns targeted in the literature include active trading, the disposition effect, paying more attention to the past performance of mutual funds than to fees, familiarity bias, mania and panic, momentum investing, naïve diversification, noise trading, and underdiversification.

Active Trading

In "Trading is Hazardous to Your Wealth: The Common Stock Investment Performance of Individual Investors," Brad M. Barber and Terrance Odean demonstrate the pitfalls of active

---

[10] Jonathan Skinner, "Are You Sure You're Saving Enough for Retirement?" *Journal of Economic Perspectives* 21, no. 3 (Summer 2007): 59–80. Available by subscription from EBSCO, http://search.ebscohost.com/ (accessed January 5, 2010). Also available from http://www.dartmouth.edu/~jskinner/documents/SkinnerAreyouSure.pdf (accessed January 15, 2010).

trading.[11] According to their study, active traders underperform the market. Active trading correlates with overconfidence. For example, in "Boys Will Be Boys: Gender, Overconfidence, and Common Stock Investment," Barber and Odean find a correlation between male overconfidence and excessive trading, particularly when comparing single men and single women.[12] Because women are less likely to indulge in excessive trading, they outperform men. In "Online Investors: Do the Slow Die First?" Barber and Odean determine that investors who use traditional brokers, remaining in touch with them by telephone, achieve better results than online traders, who damage their performance by trading more actively and speculatively.[13]

Disposition Effect

The disposition effect is the tendency of investors to sell winning positions and to hold onto losing positions. In his study of this effect, Terrance Odean poses the question: "Are Investors Reluctant to Realize Their Losses?"[14] He answers in the affirmative, demonstrating that the disposition effect is widely operative and that this investment strategy is counterproductive. According to Odean's study, in the months following the sale of winning investments, these investments continue to outperform the losing ones still held in the investment portfolio, an outcome exactly the opposite of that intended. Loss-averse investors sell high-performing investments hoping to recoup their losses on poor performers but, in fact, achieve the reverse. In "Myopic Loss Aversion and the Equity Risk Premium," Shlomo Benartzi and Richard H. Thaler, business school professors at the University of California Los Angeles and the University of Chicago, respectively, coin the term "myopic loss aversion" to describe the

[11] Brad M. Barber and Terrance Odean, "Trading Is Hazardous to Your Wealth: The Common Stock Investment Performance of Individual Investors," *Journal of Finance* 55, no. 2 (April 2000): 773–806. Available by subscription from JSTOR, http://www.jstor.org/stable/222522 (accessed December 10, 2009). Also available from http://faculty.haas.berkeley.edu/odean/Papers%20current%20versions/Individual_Investor_Performance_Final.pdf (accessed January 15, 2010).
[12] Brad M. Barber and Terrance Odean, "Boys Will Be Boys: Gender, Overconfidence, and Common Stock Investment," *Quarterly Journal of Economics* 116, no. 1 (February 2001): 261–92. Available by subscription from JSTOR, http://www.jstor.org/stable/2696449 (accessed December 10, 2009). Also available from http://faculty.gsm.ucdavis.edu/~bmbarber/Paper%20Folder/QJE%20BoysWillBeBoys.pdf (accessed January 15, 2010).
[13] Brad M. Barber and Terrance Odean, "Online Investors: Do the Slow Die First?" Special issue, *Review of Financial Studies* 15, no. 2 (2002): 455–87. Available by subscription from JSTOR, http://www.jstor.org/stable/2696785 (accessed December 10, 2009). Also available from http://faculty.haas.berkeley.edu/odean/Papers%20current%20versions/Online%20RFS.pdf (accessed January 15, 2010).
[14] Terrance Odean, "Are Investors Reluctant To Realize Their Losses?" *Journal of Finance* 53, no. 5 (October 1998): 1775–98. Available by subscription from JSTOR, http://www.jstor.org/stable/117424 (accessed December 10, 2009). Also available from http://faculty.haas.berkeley.edu/odean/Papers%20current%20versions/AreInvestorsReluctant.pdf (accessed January 15, 2010).

tendency of loss-averse investors—even if long-term investors—to evaluate their portfolios frequently.[15] The authors consider the long-term investors' focus on short-term results an unfortunate form of myopia applied to investing.

Paying More Attention to the Past Returns of Mutual Funds than to Fees

In "On Persistence in Mutual Fund Performance," Mark M. Carhart, former professor of finance at the University of Southern California, concludes that expense ratios, transaction costs, and load fees—costs that investors tend to disregard—all harm mutual-fund returns.[16] Such fees are associated with actively managed funds, in which the portfolio manager has discretion over purchases, in contrast to index funds, which mirror a benchmark index. Despite the popularity of actively managed funds, Carhart sees no evidence that portfolio managers are particularly skilled or informed, characteristics that would justify additional fees. Nevertheless, a key finding of another study indicates that full disclosure of these active management fees does not deter investors from selecting this type of fund. In their article, "Why Does the Law of One Price Fail? An Experiment on Index Mutual Funds," by James J. Choi, of Yale School of Management, David Laibson of Harvard's Department of Economics, and Brigitte C. Madrian, of Harvard's Kennedy School of Government, report that investors disregard the costs of actively managed plans, focusing instead on annualized returns, which do not predict future performance.[17] The attention paid to past performance is a behavior that leads to misguided choices. The authors find no indication that nonportfolio services justify the higher fees their managers charge investors. Moreover, they find that investors with high financial literacy tend to pay low fees.

---

[15] Shlomo Benartzi and Richard H. Thaler, "Myopic Loss Aversion and the Equity Risk Premium," *Quarterly Journal of Economics* 110, no. 1 (February 1995): 73–92. Available by subscription from JSTOR, http://www.jstor.org/stable/2118511 (accessed December 10, 2009); Shlomo Benartzi and Richard H. Thaler, "Risk Aversion or Myopia? Choices in Repeated Gambles and Retirement Investments," *Management Science* 45, no. 3 (March 1999): 364–81. Available from several vendors by subscription, including JSTOR, http://www.jstor.org/stable/2634883 (accessed December 10, 2009).

[16] Mark M. Carhart, "On Persistence in Mutual Fund Performance," *Journal of Finance* 52, no. 1 (March 1997): 57–82. Available by subscription from JSTOR, http://www.jstor.org/stable/2329556 (accessed January 5, 2010).

[17] James J. Choi, David Laibson, and Brigitte C. Madrian, "Why Does the Law of One Price Fail? An Experiment on Index Mutual Funds," *Review of Financial Studies* 23, no. 4 (April 2010): 1405. Available by subscription from National Bureau of Economic Research, http://www.nber.org/papers/w12261.pdf (accessed June 30, 2010). Also available from Oxford Journals, http://rfs.oxfordjournals.org/cgi/content/ full/hhp097v1 (accessed January 25, 2010).

Familiarity Bias

People prefer to invest in what is familiar, favoring their own country, region, state, and company. Behavioral finance specialists characterize this preference as "familiarity bias." In "Familiarity Breeds Investment," Gur Huberman, a professor of behavioral finance at Columbia University's Graduate School of Business, finds that in 49 out of 50 states, investors are more likely to hold shares of their local Regional Bell Operating Company (RBOC) than of any other single RBOC.[18] The preference of investors for companies from their region is a narrow form of geographic bias; preference for domestic companies over international ones is a widely held preference known as "equity home bias." In "Understanding the Equity Home Bias: Evidence from Survey Data," Norman Strong, of the University of Manchester in the United Kingdom, and Xinzhong Xu, affiliated with Peking University, investigate the equity-home-bias puzzle—why do investors tend to favor their own country's equities, despite the advantages of international diversification?[19] However, Strong and Xu argue that, by itself, investors' relative optimism about the home market cannot explain equity home bias. In their view, fund sponsors who constrain fund managers or measure their performance against domestic benchmarks may influence fund managers to invest in domestic equities.

A widespread and particularly dangerous form of familiarity bias is employees' preference for investing in their employer's stock. Employees already have a stake in the performance of their companies without including company shares in their investment portfolios. Not only does concentration in one asset violate the principle of portfolio diversification, but, if employees devote a large portion of their portfolios to their own company's shares, they run the risk of compounding their suffering if the company does poorly: first, in loss of compensation and job security, and second, in loss of retirement savings. This is exactly what happened to employees at Enron and Fannie Mae, when Enron filed for bankruptcy in 2001 and when Fannie Mae was placed into government conservatorship in 2008. In "Are Empowerment and Education Enough? Underdiversification in 401(k) Plans," James J. Choi, David Laibson, and Brigitte C. Madrian, who at the time of publication were professors at Yale, Harvard, and the University of

---

[18] Gur Huberman, "Familiarity Breeds Investment," *Review of Financial Studies* 14, no. 3 (Autumn 2001): 659–80. Available by subscription from JSTOR, http://www.jstor.org/stable/2696769 (accessed December 10, 2009).
[19] Norman Strong and Xinzhong Xu, "Understanding the Equity Home Bias: Evidence from Survey Data," *Review of Economics and Statistics* 85, no. 2 (May 2003): 307–12. Available by subscription from JSTOR, http://www.jstor.org/stable/3211582 (accessed December 10, 2009).

Pennsylvania, respectively, contend that employees invest in company stock for a variety of reasons, including familiarity bias, loyalty to their employers, naive-diversification strategies, and passivity.[20] Employers share some of the blame for these patterns, encouraging such behavior through employee stock-ownership plans (ESOPs) and employers' matching contributions. The preference for glamour stocks (high-growth, well-known, trendy stocks), another form of familiarity bias, is discussed in the following section on growth investing.

Manias and Panics

Financial mania is the rapid rise in the price of an asset, reflecting a high degree of collective enthusiasm or exuberance regarding that asset's prospects. Because a bubble inflates rapidly and is not durable, it is a common metaphor for financial mania. When the bubble bursts, the price of the asset plunges, setting off a panic. In "Financial Manias and Panics: A Socioeconomic Perspective," York University economist Brenda Spotton Visano uses sociologists' theories to shed light on the phenomena of mania and panic.[21] Visano describes financial mania as the "gradual spreading of speculative euphoria—one that becomes increasingly intense."[22] She explains that mania occurs before, and panic occurs after, "the peak of the business cycle spawned by revolutionary innovation."[23] Referring to sociological theories, Visano traces the progression of financial speculation and innovation from "optimistic uncertainty" to a "swell of speculative excitement" to "apparent and estimable" innovation. Unfounded optimism can lead to eventual distress and possible panic. In the past 10 years, two instances of mania followed by panic have severely harmed investors: the bursting of the dot-com bubble in 2000 and the housing crisis, which became acute in 2008 and is continuing. A diversified portfolio, including fixed-income securities, would have mitigated the impact of these crises on investment portfolios.

---

[20] James J. Choi, David Laibson, and Brigitte C. Madrian, "Are Empowerment and Education Enough? Underdiversification in 401(k) Plans," *Brookings Papers on Economic Activity* 2 (2005): 151–98. Available by subscription from JSTOR, http://www.jstor.org/stable/3805120 (accessed December 10, 2009) and Muse, https://muse.jhu.edu/journals/brookings_papers_on_economic_activity/v2005/2005.2choi.pdf (accessed January 15, 2010).

[21] Brenda Spotton Visano, "Financial Manias and Panics: A Socioeconomic Perspective," *American Journal of Economics and Sociology* 61, no. 4 (October 2002): 801–27. Available by subscription from JSTOR, http://www.jstor.org/stable/3487980 (accessed January 5, 2010).

[22] Visano, "Financial Manias and Panics," 816.

[23] Visano, "Financial Manias and Panics," 809.

Momentum Investing

Momentum investing is an investment strategy whereby the investor buys securities with high recent returns and sells those with low recent returns, in the expectation that past trends will continue. Mohacsy and Lefer equate momentum investing, which is a manifestation of magical thinking and herd behavior, with the Greater Fool Theory.[24] Momentum investing can give rise to speculative bubbles, such as the dot-com bubble of the second half of the 1990s. In the article, "A Unified Theory of Underreaction, Momentum Trading, and Overreaction in Asset Markets," Harrison Hong and Jeremy C. Stein, who were business school professors at Stanford and the Massachusetts Institute of Technology, respectively, when they wrote this article, show that short-run momentum can lead to long-run reversals when stock prices overshoot their intrinsic value.[25] They distinguish between "newswatchers," who focus on privately observed information, and "momentum traders," who seek to take advantage of a price trend. Both are subject to bounded rationality,[26] not taking into account all publicly available information. Newswatchers focus on information that may spread slowly, giving momentum traders an opportunity to step in and to trigger an overreaction followed by a reversal. Slow information diffusion is characteristic of small-cap stocks with low analyst coverage.

Naive Diversification

In their study, "Naive Diversification Strategies in Defined Contribution Saving Plans," Benartzi and Thaler explore the tendency of investors in defined contribution retirement plans to take the "naive diversification" approach toward asset allocation.[27] In other words, if given *n*

---

[24] Mohacsy and Lefer, "Money and Sentiment: A Psychodynamic Approach to Behavioral Finance."

[25] Harrison Hong and Jeremy C. Stein, "A Unified Theory of Underreaction, Momentum Trading, and Overreaction in Asset Markets," *Journal of Finance* 54, no. 6 (December 1999): 2143–84, http://www.economics.harvard.edu/ faculty/stein/files/UnifiedTheory.pdf (accessed May 20, 2010).

[26] According to *BusinessDictionary.com*, "bounded rationality" is the "concept that decision makers (irrespective of their level of intelligence) have to work under three unavoidable constraints: (1) only limited, often unreliable, information is available regarding possible alternatives and their consequences, (2) [the] human mind has only limited capacity to evaluate and process the information that is available, and (3) only a limited amount of time is available to make a decision. Therefore, even individuals who intend to make rational choices are bound to make satisficing (rather than maximizing or optimizing) choices in complex situations." "Bounded Rationality," *BusinessDictionary. com*, http://www.businessdictionary.com/definition/bounded-rationality.html (accessed June 18, 2010).

[27] Shlomo Benartzi and Richard H. Thaler, "Naive Diversification Strategies in Defined Contribution Saving Plans," *American Economic Review* 91, no. 1 (March 2001): 79–98. Available by subscription from JSTOR, http://www. jstor.org/stable/2677899 (accessed December 10, 2009). Also available from http://faculty.chicagobooth.edu/ richard.thaler/research/pdf/ (accessed January 15, 2010).

options, investors allocate their assets proportionally among them, so that each option receives *1/n* of the total. The authors maintain that, although naive diversification is not necessarily a bad approach for unsophisticated investors, this method may prove costly if the employer provides a poor selection of choices. The study implies that employers should design retirement plans carefully, to produce a scenario in which naive diversification becomes an effective strategy.

Noise Trading

As a technical term, "noise" refers to false signals and short-term volatility that obscure the overall trend. Therefore, "noise trading" describes the activities of "an investor who makes decisions regarding buy and sell trades without the use of fundamental data. These investors generally have poor timing, follow trends, and overreact to good and bad news."[28] In "All that Glitters: The Effect of Attention and News on the Buying Behavior of Individual and Institutional Investors," Brad M. Barber and Terrance Odean show that although individual investors are net buyers of attention-grabbing stocks—stocks that are in the news or that experience abnormal one-day returns or trading volumes—these stocks subsequently do not perform as well as the stocks that the same investors decided to sell.[29] This research suggests that day trading is not a worthwhile activity.

Underdiversification

Behavioral finance theorists do not have a monopoly on identifying investing mistakes. Inadequate portfolio diversification, for example, violates the principles of best practice set out in Modern Portfolio Theory, which Nobel Prize–winning economist Harry Markowitz developed in the 1950s. Meir Statman, a professor of finance at Santa Clara University, explored the lack of diversification in U.S. investors' equity portfolios. Although mean-variance portfolio theory recommends that portfolios hold at least 300 stocks, the average investor actually holds only three or four, representing an extremely underdiversified portfolio. The typical investor's

---

[28] "Noise Trader," *Investopedia*, http://www.investopedia.com/terms/n/noisetrader.asp (accessed June 18, 2010).
[29] Brad M. Barber and Terrance Odean, "All that Glitters: The Effect of Attention and News on the Buying Behavior of Individual and Institutional Investors," *Review of Financial Studies* 21, no. 2 (April 2008): 785–818. Available by subscription from Oxford Journals, http://rfs.oxfordjournals.org/cgi/reprint/21/2/785 (accessed January 5, 2010). Also available from http://faculty.haas.berkeley.edu/odean/papers/Attention/All%20that%20Glitters.pdf (accessed January 16, 2010).

concentration in employer, large-capitalization, and domestic stocks also works against the advantages of diversification.[30]

A contrarian view of portfolio diversification is found in "Portfolio Concentration and the Performance of Individual Investors," by finance professors Zoran Ivković, of Michigan State University, Clemens Sialm, of the University of Texas at Austin, and Scott Weisbenner, of the University of Illinois at Urbana-Champaign.[31] The authors determine that, contrary to conventional financial advice recommending investment in well-diversified portfolios, some individual investors (particularly those from households with large portfolios) achieve superior returns by concentrating their investments in a few stocks. Financial returns in excess of the norm correlate with local stocks, stocks not included in the S&P 500 index (small capitalization stocks), and stocks with less analyst coverage.

OTHER BEHAVIORAL PATTERNS

Behavioral finance specialists have also analyzed other investment patterns that are the frequent object of debate. Two of them are the appropriateness of annuity investing and the relative merit of the growth vs. value styles of investing.

Annuity Investing

To suggest that all annuities are poor investments is unjustified. However, according to the article, "Who Chooses Annuities? An Experimental Investigation of the Role of Gender, Framing and Defaults," by Julie R. Agnew, Lisa R. Anderson, and Lisa R. Szykman, of the College of William and Mary, and Jeffrey R. Gerlach of the Massachusetts Institute of Technology, annuities offer modest returns for a given level of risk. The authors note that annuities attract a middle-class, relatively well-educated, and predominantly female clientele, motivated by affective (emotional) factors, such as trust, familiarity, and loss aversion. Examining how women and men differ in their approach to the choice of whether to purchase an annuity or to invest on their own, and controlling for risk aversion and financial literacy, the

---

[30] Meir Statman, "The Diversification Puzzle," *Financial Analysts Journal* 60, no. 4 (July–August 2004): 44–53. Available by subscription from JSTOR, http://www.jstor.org/stable/4480587 (accessed January 5, 2010).
[31] Zoran Ivković, Clemens Sialm, and Scott Weisbenner, "Portfolio Concentration and the Performance of Individual Investors," *Journal of Financial and Quantitative Analysis* 43, no. 3 (September 2008): 613–56. Available by subscription from EBSCO, http://search.ebscohost.com/ (accessed January 5, 2010).

authors find that women are more likely than men to purchase an annuity.[32] Although men tend to overconfidence in their investing prowess, perhaps this trait may have a benefit; instead, women settle for modest annuity-like returns.

Growth Investing

In the "value style" of investing, an investor buys out-of-favor stocks with low price-to-earnings and price-to-book value ratios, stocks that the investor believes are trading below their intrinsic value. "Growth style" describes an approach to investing that focuses on high-growth stocks, even if they have high price-to-earning ratios. To imply that growth investing is an investing mistake would be an overstatement. However, an investor's choice of growth- or value-investing styles may affect the outcome of his or her results. In their article, "Value and Growth Investing: Review and Update," Louis K. C. Chan and Josef Lakonishok, both finance professors at the University of Illinois at Urbana-Champaign, maintain that value investing generates superior returns to growth investing, particularly for small-capitalization stocks.[33] The authors' assertion carries a significant caveat: before 1990, value stocks had a superior performance, but their performance reversed during the 1990s. The authors attribute the reversal during that decade to investors' excessive enthusiasm for technology, media, and telecom stocks that defied economic logic.

The authors suggest that investors tend to underestimate the ability of value stocks to rebound and to overestimate the ability of glamour stocks to maintain above-average growth. Investors' overly optimistic tendency to project rapid growth rates into the future may have a cost, which is exacerbated by financial management agencies' practice of delegating investment decisions to professional money managers. Analysts, money managers, and pension plan executives often promote or invest in glamour stocks for a variety of inappropriate reasons that may betray the interests of their clients. Analysts may have conflicts of interests, relative to investment banking, leading them to recommend growth stocks; money managers may offer advice to investors that promote their own careers; and excitement over emerging technologies

---

[32] Julie R. Agnew, Lisa R. Anderson, Jeffrey R. Gerlach, and Lisa R. Szykman, "Who Chooses Annuities? An Experimental Investigation of the Role of Gender, Framing and Defaults," *American Economic Review* 98, no. 2 (May 2008): 418–22, http://lrande.people.wm.edu/links/AERP&P2008.pdf (accessed May 13, 2010).
[33] Louis K. C. Chan and Josef Lakonishok, "Value and Growth Investing: Review and Update," *Financial Analysts Journal* 60, no. 1 (January–February 2004): 71–86. Available by subscription: http://www.jstor.org/stable/4480542

may lead advisers to select glamorous, but unwise, investments. Whether investor psychology or agency self-interest is the cause, excessive investment in these stocks may drive up the prices of growth stocks beyond their intrinsic value. This type of mispricing may persist for a long time but will not continue indefinitely; unappreciated value stocks eventually recover. Over time, growth stocks fail to meet optimistic expectations, while value stocks exceed pessimistic expectations.

CONCLUSION

By identifying and explaining patterns of poor investor decision making, behavioral finance theory has contributed to our understanding of investment behavior. In contrast to rational expectations theory, behavioral finance highlights the role of social, cognitive, and emotional factors in investing. Consequently, this field can help educate investors—an essential means of preventing investors from committing a predictable series of mistakes. In addition, the findings of behavioral scientists suggest that investors need streamlined, transparent investment disclosure, particularly in graphical format. Investment professionals should take into account the findings of behavioral finance when they advise clients and monitor their accounts. Finally, many scholars strongly advocate that employers improve their design of retirement plans to diversified, simple fund options and automatic enrollment provisions that require employees to opt out, in order to encourage participation.

(accessed January 12, 2010). Also available: http://www.lsvasset.com/pdf/Value-Review.pdf (accessed January 26, 2010).

BIBLIOGRAPHY

Agnew, Julie R., Lisa R. Anderson, Jeffrey R. Gerlach, and Lisa R. Szykman. "Who Chooses
    Annuities? An Experimental Investigation of the Role of Gender, Framing and Defaults."
    American Economic Review 98, no. 2 (May 2008): 418–22. http://lrande.people.wm.edu/
    http://lrande.people.wm.edu/links/AERP&P2008.pdf (accessed May 13, 2010).

Barber, Brad M., and Terrance Odean. "All that Glitters: The Effect of Attention and News on
    the Buying Behavior of Individual and Institutional Investors." *Review of Financial
    Studies* 21, no. 2 (April 2008): 785–818. Available by subscription: http://rfs.
    oxfordjournals.org/cgi/reprint/21/2/785 (January 5, 2010). Also available: http://faculty.
    haas.berkeley.edu/odean/papers/Attention/All%20that%20Glitters.pdf (accessed January
    16, 2010).

Barber, Brad M., and Terrance Odean. "Boys Will Be Boys: Gender, Overconfidence, and
    Common Stock Investment." *Quarterly Journal of Economics* 116, no. 1 (February
    2001): 261–92. Available by subscription: http://www.jstor.org/stable/2696449 (accessed
    December 10, 2009). Also available: http://faculty.gsm.ucdavis.edu/~bmbarber/Paper%
    20Folder/QJE%20BoysWillBeBoys.pdf (accessed January 15, 2010).

Barber, Brad M., and Terrance Odean. "The Courage of Misguided Convictions." *Financial
    Analysts Journal* 55, no. 6 (November–December 1999): 41–55. Available by
    subscription: http://www.jstor.org/stable/4480208 (accessed December 10, 2009). Also
    available: http://faculty.haas.berkeley.edu/odean/Papers%20current%20versions/FAJ%
    20NovDec99%20Barber%20and%20Odean.pdf (accessed January 15, 2010).

Barber, Brad M., and Terrance Odean. "Online Investors: Do the Slow Die First?" Special issue,
    Review of Financial Studies 15, no. 2 (2002): 455–87. Available by subscription:
    http://www.jstor.org/stable/2696785 (accessed December 10, 2009). Also available:
    http://faculty.haas.berkeley.edu/odean/Papers%20current%20versions/Online%20RFS.
    pdf (accessed January 15, 2010).

Barber, Brad M., and Terrance Odean. "Trading is Hazardous to Your Wealth: The Common
    Stock Investment Performance of Individual Investors." *Journal of Finance* 55, no. 2
    (April 2000): 773–806. Available by subscription: http://www.jstor.org/stable/222522
    (December 10, 2009). Also available: http://faculty.haas.berkeley.edu/odean/Papers%
    20current%20versions/Individual_Investor_Performance_Final.pdf (accessed January 15,
    2010).

Benartzi, Shlomo, and Richard H. Thaler. "Myopic Loss Aversion and the Equity Risk
    Premium." *Quarterly Journal of Economics* 110, no. 1 (February 1995): 73–92.
    Available by subscription: http://www.jstor.org/stable/2118511 (accessed December 10,
    2009).

Benartzi, Shlomo, and Richard H. Thaler. "Naive Diversification Strategies in Defined
    Contribution Saving Plans." *American Economic Review* 91, no. 1 (March 2001): 79–98.

Available by subscription: http://www.jstor.org/stable/2677899 (accessed December 10, 2009). Also available: http://faculty.chicagobooth.edu/richard.thaler/research/pdf/ DiversificationStrategies.pdf (accessed January 15, 2010).

Carhart, Mark M. "On Persistence in Mutual Fund Performance." *Journal of Finance* 52, no. 1 (March 1997): 57–82. Available by subscription: http://www.jstor.org/stable/2329556 (accessed January 5, 2010).

Chan, Louis K. C., and Josef Lakonishok. "Value and Growth Investing: Review and Update." *Financial Analysts Journal* 60, no. 1 (January–February 2004): 71–86. Available by subscription: http://www.jstor.org/stable/4480542 (accessed January 12, 2010). Also available: http://www.lsvasset.com/pdf/Value-Review.pdf (accessed January 26, 2010).

Choi, James J., David Laibson, and Brigitte C. Madrian. "Are Empowerment and Education Enough? Underdiversification in 401(k) Plans." *Brookings Papers on Economic Activity*, no. 2 (2005): 151–98. Available by subscription: http://www.jstor.org/stable/3805120 (accessed December 10, 2009) and https://muse.jhu.edu/journals/brookings_papers_ on_economic_activity/v2005/2005.2choi.pdf (accessed January 15, 2010).

Choi, James J., David Laibson, and Brigitte C. Madrian. "Why Does the Law of One Price Fail? An Experiment on Index Mutual Funds." *Review of Financial Studies* 23, no. 4 (April 2010). Available by subscription: http://www.nber.org/papers/w12261.pdf (accessed June 30, 2010). Also available: http://rfs.oxfordjournals.org/cgi/content/full/hhp097v1 (accessed January 25, 2010).

Guiso, Luigi, Paola Sapienza, and Luigi Zingales. "Trusting the Stock Market." *Journal of Finance* 63, no. 6 (December 2008): 2557–2600. http://www.bus.wisc.edu/finance/ Meyferth/Fedenia/Articles/Guiso%20Sapienza%20Zingales%202007.pdf (accessed May 19, 2010).

Hong, Harrison, and Jeremy C. Stein. "A Unified Theory of Underreaction, Momentum Trading, and Overreaction in Asset Markets." *Journal of Finance* 54, no. 6 (December 1999): 2143–84. http://www.economics.harvard.edu/faculty/stein/files/UnifiedTheory.pdf (accessed May 20, 2010).

Huberman, Gur. "Familiarity Breeds Investment." *Review of Financial Studies* 14, no. 3 (Autumn 2001): 659–80. Available by subscription: http://www.jstor.org/stable/2696769 (accessed December 10, 2009).

Ivković, Zoran, Clemens Sialm, and Scott Weisbenner. "Portfolio Concentration and the Performance of Individual Investors." *Journal of Financial and Quantitative Analysis* 43, no. 3 (September 2008): 613–56. Available by subscription: http://search.ebscohost.com/ (accessed January 5, 2010).

Kahneman, Daniel, and Mark W. Riepe. "Aspects of Investor Psychology." Journal of Portfolio Management 24, no. 4 (Summer 1998): 52. Available by subscription: http://find.

galegroup.com/gtx/infomark.do?&contentSet=IAC-Documents&type=retrieve&tabID =T002&prodId=ITOF&docId=A21046822&source=gale&srcprod=ITOF&userGroup Name=loc_main&version=1.0 (accessed June 29, 2010).

Kahneman, Daniel, and Amos Tversky, "Prospect Theory: An Analysis of Decision under Risk," *Econometrica*, 47, no. 2 (March 1979): 279. Available by subscription: http://www.jstor. org/stable/1914185 (accessed June 15, 2010).

Mitchell, Olivia S., and Stephen P. Utkus. "Lessons from Behavioral Finance for Retirement Plan Design." In *Pension Design and Structure: New Lessons from Behavioral Finance*, edited by Olivia S. Mitchell and Stephen P. Utkus, 3–41. Oxford, UK: Oxford University Press, 2004. Version available at http://fic.wharton.upenn.edu/ fic/papers/03/0334.pdf (accessed June 15, 2010).

Mohacsy, Ildiko, and Heidi Lefer. "Money and Sentiment: A Psychodynamic Approach to Behavioral Finance." *Journal of the American Academy of Psychoanalysis and Dynamic Psychiatry* 35, no. 3 (Fall 2007): 455–75. Available by subscription from a number of vendors, including: http://proquest.umi.com/login (accessed January 13, 2010).

Odean, Terrance. "Are Investors Reluctant to Realize Their Losses?" *Journal of Finance* 53, no. 5 (October 1998): 1775–98. Available by subscription: http://www.jstor.org/stable/ 117424 (accessed December 10, 2009). Also available: http://faculty.haas.berkeley.edu/ odean/Papers%20current%20versions/AreInvestorsReluctant.pdf (accessed January 15, 2010).

Pressman, Steven. "On Financial Frauds and Their Causes: Investor Overconfidence." *American Journal of Economics and Sociology* 57, no. 4 (October 1998): 405–21. Available by subscription: http://www.jstor.org/stable/3487115 (accessed December 10, 2009).

Skinner, Jonathan. "Are You Sure You're Saving Enough for Retirement?" *Journal of Economic Perspectives* 21, no. 3 (Summer 2007): 59–80. Available by subscription: http://search. ebscohost.com/ (accessed January 5, 2010). Also available: http://www.dartmouth.edu/~ jskinner/documents/SkinnerAreyouSure.pdf (accessed January 15, 2010).

Statman, Meir. "The Diversification Puzzle." *Financial Analysts Journal* 60, no. 4 (July–August 2004): 44–53. Available by subscription: http://www.jstor.org/stable/4480587 (accessed January 5, 2010).

Strong, Norman, and Xinzhong Xu. "Understanding the Equity Home Bias: Evidence from Survey Data." *Review of Economics and Statistics* 85, no. 2 (May 2003): 307–12. Available by subscription: http://www.jstor.org/stable/3211582 (accessed December 10, 2009).

Van Rooij, Maarten, Annamaria Lusardi, and Rob Alessie. "Financial Literacy and Stock Market Participation." National Bureau of Economic Research Working Paper 13565, October 2007. http://www.nber.org/papers/w13565 (accessed May 21, 2010).

Visano, Brenda Spotton. "Financial Manias and Panics: A Socioeconomic Perspective."
    American Journal of Economics and Sociology 61, no. 4 (October 2002): 801–27.
    Available by subscription: http://www.jstor.org/stable/3487980 (accessed January 5,
    2010).